Quilter's DESK DIARY 2015

Welcome to 2015

Stay organized in style with *The Quilter's Desk Diary 2015*. Illustrated throughout with beautiful photographs of inspirational quilts from the most talented of quiltmakers, each week-to-view diary page has plenty of room for your own personal notes. If you want to find out more about any of the quiltmakers featured, turn to the back of the diary for information about them and the books they have written.

D&C
David and Charles
www.stitchcraftcreate.co.uk

29
Monday

30
Tuesday

31
Wednesday

New Year's Day

1
Thursday

2
Friday

3
Saturday

4
Sunday

JANUARY						
M	T	W	T	F	S	S
			1	2	3	4
5	6	7	8	9	10	11
12	13	14	15	16	17	18
19	20	21	22	23	24	25
26	27	28	29	30	31	

Building Blocks
Improvised quilts are bold, bright and colourful when sewn by an improv-master like Lucie Summers. In her book *Quilt Improv*, Lucie shows how you can use her collection of building blocks to create improvised quilts of your very own.

January

5
Monday

6
Tuesday

7
Wednesday

8
Thursday

9
Friday

10
Saturday

11
Sunday

Wrapped up Warm

Janet Bolton is known worldwide for her naive appliqué. Her deceptively simple pictures are admired by all. Fabric is her main source of inspiration, and the juxtaposition of texture, weave, colour and pattern is essential in her work, as in this picture inspired by one of her grandchildren. Janet's Folk Art Collage masterclass can be found in *The Quiltmakers*.

JANUARY

M	T	W	T	F	S	S
			1	2	3	4
5	6	7	8	9	10	11
12	13	14	15	16	17	18
19	20	21	22	23	24	25
26	27	28	29	30	31	

12
Monday

13
Tuesday

14
Wednesday

15
Thursday

16
Friday

17
Saturday

18
Sunday

Friendship in Paradise

Dessert Rolls™ are delicious bundles of pre-cut fabrics available from Moda. Each perfectly coordinated collection of 20.5in-strips, cut across the fabric width, can produce a stunning quilt top when working the designs from *Dessert Roll Quilts* by Pam and Nicky Lintott. The Paradise quilt, which utilizes a traditional Friendship Star block, is just one of 12 gorgeous new quilt designs they have specially created to inspire you to try Dessert Rolls™ for yourself.

JANUARY

M	T	W	T	F	S	S
			1	2	3	4
5	6	7	8	9	10	11
12	13	14	15	16	17	18
19	20	21	22	23	24	25
26	27	28	29	30	31	

January

Martin Luther King Day (US)

19
Monday

20
Tuesday

21
Wednesday

22
Thursday

23
Friday

24
Saturday

25
Sunday

Street Skyline

Home Quilt Home by Janet Clare is an inspiring collection of designs for quilts, wall hangings and cushions all based on the idea of the home. For this quilt, Janet thought it would be fun to give quiltmakers the chance to play at being an architect or town planner, so she came up with a variety of houses, roofs and chimneys that can be mixed and matched to celebrate life in town.

JANUARY

M	T	W	T	F	S	S
			1	2	3	4
5	6	7	8	9	10	11
12	13	14	15	16	17	18
19	20	21	22	23	24	25
26	27	28	29	30	31	

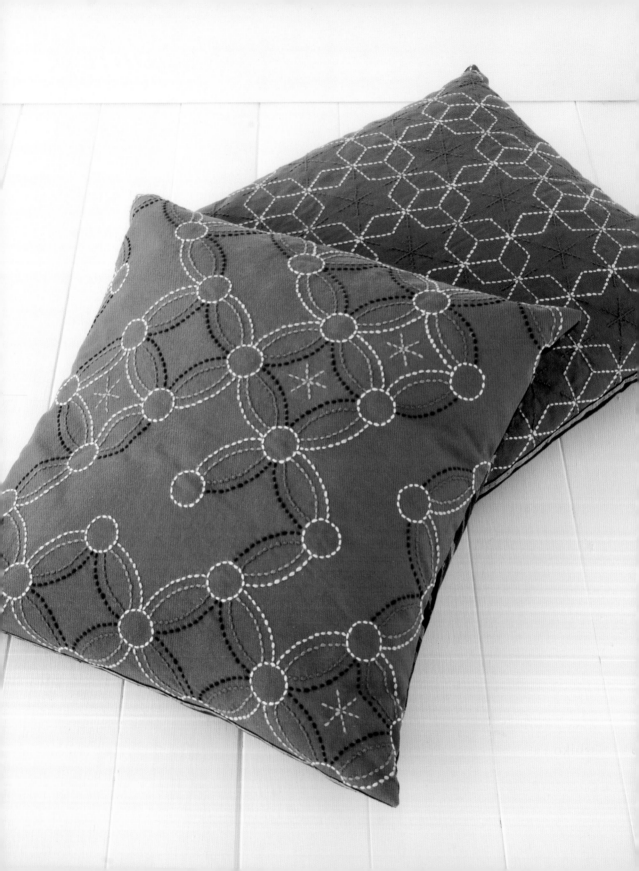

January/February

26
Monday

27
Tuesday

28
Wednesday

29
Thursday

30
Friday

31
Saturday

1
Sunday

FEBRUARY						
M	T	W	T	F	S	S
						1
2	3	4	5	6	7	8
9	10	11	12	13	14	15
16	17	18	19	20	21	22
23	24	25	26	27	28	

Sashiko Patterns

The sashiko patterns used on these large cushions were adapted from vintage stencils for *katazome* dyeing, a traditional Japanese technique. Susan Briscoe has plenty more ideas to inspire you to get creative with sashiko stitches in *Japanese Sashiko Inspirations*.

February

2
Monday

3
Tuesday

4
Wednesday

5
Thursday

6
Friday

7
Saturday

8
Sunday

Medallion Pinwheel

Making Welsh Quilts by Mary Jenkins and Clare Claridge explores the history of traditional Welsh quilting. The inspiration for this piece was a 19th century wool quilt which is now in the Collection of the Quilters' Guild of the British Isles. The original was made from turquoise blue petticoat fabrics and the remains of a Paisley quilt. Clare's chosen colourway is completely different, yet no less striking.

		FEBRUARY				
M	T	W	T	F	S	S
						1
2	3	4	5	6	7	8
9	10	11	12	13	14	15
16	17	18	19	20	21	22
23	24	25	26	27	28	

February

9
Monday

10
Tuesday

11
Wednesday

12
Thursday

13
Friday

Valentine's Day

14
Saturday

15
Sunday

Yo-Yo Heart

A simple-to-stitch patchwork heart makes a great alternative
to a Valentine's Day card, and it's an ideal way to try out a new
technique, like these sweet little yo-yo embellishments. Helen
Philipps' *Pretty Patchwork Gifts* is full of beautiful projects made
in fresh, contemporary fabrics that are ideal for giving.

FEBRUARY						
M	T	W	T	F	S	S
						1
2	3	4	5	6	7	8
9	10	11	12	13	14	15
16	17	18	19	20	21	22
23	24	25	26	27	28	

February

16
Monday

17
Tuesday

18
Wednesday

19
Thursday

20
Friday

21
Saturday

22
Sunday

Flower Power

In *Quick Quilts with Rulers*, best-selling Jelly Roll™ quilt authors Pam and Nicky Lintott present 18 stunning quilt designs that can be made using one of three rulers for quick and easy patchwork. This bright and cheerful quilt, pieced from gorgeous Kaffe Fassett fabrics, is perfect for getting to grips with a Multi-Size 2 Peaks in 1 Triangle ruler, as it is just 35 repeated blocks with a narrow border.

FEBRUARY

M	T	W	T	F	S	S
						1
2	3	4	5	6	7	8
9	10	11	12	13	14	15
16	17	18	19	20	21	22
23	24	25	26	27	28	

23
Monday

24
Tuesday

25
Wednesday

26
Thursday

27
Friday

28
Saturday

1
Sunday

Carolina Lily

Lynne Edwards` *The Essential Sampler Quilt Book* provides masterclass instruction for making 40 pieced blocks using both hand and machine techniques, including this traditional block which combines pieced patchwork with appliqué. Inspiration is provided for showing how the blocks, like this one made by Barbara Ayre, can be combined to create your very own heirloom sampler quilt.

MARCH						
M	T	W	T	F	S	S
						1
2	3	4	5	6	7	8
9	10	11	12	13	14	15
16	17	18	19	20	21	22
23	24	25	26	27	28	29
30	31					

- -

2
Monday

- -

3
Tuesday

- -

4
Wednesday

- -

5
Thursday

- -

6
Friday

- -

7
Saturday

- -

8
Sunday

- -

Kaleidoscope and Jigsaw

In *Two From One Jelly Roll Quilts* Pam and Nicky Lintott show how to use just one Jelly Roll™ to make two quilts – half the fabric, but twice the inspiration. The lovely soft colours used to make the Sawtooth blocks of the Jigsaw quilt were leftover once the dark reds and dark blues were pulled out to be make its pair, the Kaleidoscope quilt – but to see that, you'll have to see Pam and Nicky's book!

		MARCH				
M	T	W	T	F	S	S
						1
2	3	4	5	6	7	8
9	10	11	12	13	14	15
16	17	18	19	20	21	22
23	24	25	26	27	28	29
30	31					

9
Monday

10
Tuesday

11
Wednesday

12
Thursday

13
Friday

14
Saturday

Mother's Day (UK)

15
Sunday

Floral Dimensions

This stunning block appears on Pauline Ineson's award-winning quilt of the same name. The roundel features three incredibly lifelike flowers – the pansy, the bell flower and the lily, and in her book, also called *Floral Dimensions*, Pauline shares the secrets of creating a total of 20 three-dimensional fabric flowers using machine appliqué.

MARCH						
M	T	W	T	F	S	S
						1
2	3	4	5	6	7	8
9	10	11	12	13	14	15
16	17	18	19	20	21	22
23	24	25	26	27	28	29
30	31					

March

16
Monday

17
Tuesday

18
Wednesday

19
Thursday

20
Friday

21
Saturday

22
Sunday

Dolly Mixtures

Tessellating patterns – identical units that interlock with one another – are a great resource for quilters as Christine Porter discovers in *Tessellation Quilts*. Here triangles are grouped together into four to make a large triangle that uses two values of each colour, and the triangle units are pieced to create diagonal lines of colour, reminiscent of a favourite British sweet – dolly mixtures!

		MARCH				
M	T	W	T	F	S	S
						1
2	3	4	5	6	7	8
9	10	11	12	13	14	15
16	17	18	19	20	21	22
23	24	25	26	27	28	29
30	31					

23
Monday

24
Tuesday

25
Wednesday

26
Thursday

27
Friday

28
Saturday

29
Sunday

Tipsy Tumblers

Pam and Nicky Lintott's book *More Layer Cake, Jelly Roll & Charm Quilts* has all the help you need to get the most from your favourite pre-cut fabric bundles. This design is a variation on one of the 14 quilt designs included, and it was quick to make, using the stack, slice, shuffle and sew method, from a layer cake pre-cut fabric pack in the all-time favourite companions of red, white and blue.

			MARCH			
M	T	W	T	F	S	S
						1
2	3	4	5	6	7	8
9	10	11	12	13	14	15
16	17	18	19	20	21	22
23	24	25	26	27	28	29
30	31					

30
Monday

31
Tuesday

1
Wednesday

2
Thursday

Good Friday (UK, Aus)

3
Friday

4
Saturday

Easter Sunday

5
Sunday

Bright Batiks

Lynne Edwards' used marbled and batik fabrics in beautiful
colours to create this striking wall hanging, which showcases
the classic Cathedral Window technique with a beautiful
border of Twisted Windows. A world-renowned expert of this
folded patchwork technique. Lynne shares her secrets for
perfecting it in her book, *Cathedral Window Quilts.*

APRIL						
M	T	W	T	F	S	S
		1	2	3	4	5
6	7	8	9	10	11	12
13	14	15	16	17	18	19
20	21	22	23	24	25	26
27	28	29	30			

April

Easter Monday (UK, Aus)

6
Monday

7
Tuesday

8
Wednesday

9
Thursday

10
Friday

11
Saturday

12
Sunday

Cherry Blossoms

The *sakura* (cherry blossom) sewing set features in *Easy Japanese Quilt Style* by Julia Davis and Anne Muxworthy, a collection of 10 stylish but simple projects inspired by Japanese fabric. With matching pincushion, needle case and scissor holder, it would make a beautiful and practical gift for a friend who loves sewing – or why not make it for yourself?

APRIL

M	T	W	T	F	S	S
		1	2	3	4	5
6	7	8	9	10	11	12
13	14	15	16	17	18	19
20	21	22	23	24	25	26
27	28	29	30			

April

13
Monday

14
Tuesday

15
Wednesday

16
Thursday

17
Friday

18
Saturday

19
Sunday

For Emma

This design by Jennifer Goldstein won third prize in the Jelly Roll™ Dream Challenge. The finished quilt is named for her little girl, Emma, who she hopes will grow up sewing with her, as Jennifer did with her own mother. All 12 prize-winning quilts can be seen in *Jelly Roll Dreams*, compiled by Pam and Nicky Lintott.

APRIL						
M	T	W	T	F	S	S
		1	2	3	4	5
6	7	8	9	10	11	12
13	14	15	16	17	18	19
20	21	22	23	24	25	26
27	28	29	30			

April

20
Monday

21
Tuesday

22
Wednesday

23
Thursday

24
Friday

Anzac Day (Aus, NZ)

25
Saturday

26
Sunday

Funky Town

The chance discovery of a black and white window fabric inspired Elizabeth Betts, author of *Beginner's Guide to Quilting*, to create her very own row of patchwork terrace houses. Elizabeth's book features 16 fresh and contemporary designs, each specially designed to introduce the basic concepts of the craft. Funky Town is an up-to-date take on the classic Schoolhouse block.

			APRIL			
M	T	W	T	F	S	S
		1	2	3	4	5
6	7	8	9	10	11	12
13	14	15	16	17	18	19
20	21	22	23	24	25	26
27	28	29	30			

27
Monday

28
Tuesday

29
Wednesday

30
Thursday

1
Friday

2
Saturday

3
Sunday

Sampler Quilt

Making a sampler quilt is an ideal way to try a variety of different techniques without ending up with a pile of unfinished samples. Skills are acquired for future projects and new techniques become unexpected favourites. Lynne Edwards' *The Essential Sampler Quilt Book* offers inspiration and techniques for making a sampler quilt just like this one, made by one of her students, Jan Evers.

MAY						
M	T	W	T	F	S	S
				1	2	3
4	5	6	7	8	9	10
11	12	13	14	15	16	17
18	19	20	21	22	23	24
25	26	27	28	29	30	31

May

4
Monday

5
Tuesday

6
Wednesday

7
Thursday

8
Friday

9
Saturday

Mother's Day (US, Aus)

10
Sunday

Daisy and Lavender

With its use of pretty, floral fabrics, appliquéd daisies and embroidered lavender flowers, this charming cushion is reminiscent of a summer garden. It is just one of many country-inspired designs from *Cushions & Quilts*, created by Jo Colwill, the founder of the highly acclaimed Cowslip Workshops, which she runs on her family's organic farm in Cornwall.

MAY

M	T	W	T	F	S	S
				1	2	3
4	5	6	7	8	9	10
11	12	13	14	15	16	17
18	19	20	21	22	23	24
25	26	27	28	29	30	31

11
Monday

12
Tuesday

13
Wednesday

14
Thursday

15
Friday

16
Saturday

17
Sunday

Twinkling Stars

This quilt design uses the warm tones so characteristic of Fig Tree designs, which is not surprising as it was designed by the founder of that company, Joanna Figueroa. The quilt's secondary pattern created by the brown triangles, makes stars appear that seem to dance and sparkle as you look at them. Joanna shares her top tips for fabric and colour selection in *The Quiltmakers*.

MAY

M	T	W	T	F	S	S
				1	2	3
4	5	6	7	8	9	10
11	12	13	14	15	16	17
18	19	20	21	22	23	24
25	26	27	28	29	30	31

18
Monday

19
Tuesday

20
Wednesday

21
Thursday

22
Friday

23
Saturday

24
Sunday

Dripping with Diamonds

When Joanna Wilczynska prepared to design her second Jelly Roll™ quilt, her aim was to create an easy and eye-catching quilt with big blocks to show off the bold colours and fabric prints. It certainly caught the eye of Pam and Nicky Lintott who chose it as one of the winning entries in their Jelly Roll™ Dream Challenge, published in their book *Jelly Roll Dreams*.

MAY

M	T	W	T	F	S	S
				1	2	3
4	5	6	7	8	9	10
11	12	13	14	15	16	17
18	19	20	21	22	23	24
25	26	27	28	29	30	31

May

25
Monday

26
Tuesday

27
Wednesday

28
Thursday

29
Friday

30
Saturday

31
Sunday

Pigs in Clover

In *Blanket Stitch Quilts*, award-winning quilter, Lynne Edwards, shares the secrets of the simple stick-and-stitch appliqué technique. She has 12 stunning projects for you to choose from, including this oh-so-cheerful cot quilt.

MAY

M	T	W	T	F	S	S
				1	2	3
4	5	6	7	8	9	10
11	12	13	14	15	16	17
18	19	20	21	22	23	24
25	26	27	28	29	30	31

June

1
Monday

2
Tuesday

3
Wednesday

4
Thursday

5
Friday

6
Saturday

7
Sunday

Stash Sack

Bring the simplicity and sophistication of Japanese style into your
home with the easy-to-make quilt collection featured in *Japanese
Quilt Inspirations*. Susan Briscoe has also included some ideas
for using up your spare blocks, such as a versatile drawstring bag
which can be made up in a variety of sizes. Based on a traditional
komebukuro (rice bag), it makes a great store for your fabric leftovers.

JUNE

M	T	W	T	F	S	S
1	2	3	4	5	6	7
8	9	10	11	12	13	14
15	16	17	18	19	20	21
22	23	24	25	26	27	28
29	30					

8
Monday

9
Tuesday

10
Wednesday

11
Thursday

12
Friday

13
Saturday

14
Sunday

Quilting 'til the Cows Come Home

Evolved from a desire to use up scraps of fabric and inspired by
the colours of the countryside and the tracks that animals make
in the fields, this design by Jo Colwill, founder of the Cowslip
Workshops in Cornwall, can be found in her book *Cushions &
Quilts*, a collection of quilting projects to decorate your home.

			JUNE			
M	T	W	T	F	S	S
1	2	3	4	5	6	7
8	9	10	11	12	13	14
15	16	17	18	19	20	21
22	23	24	25	26	27	28
29	30					

- -

15
Monday

- -

16
Tuesday

- -

17
Wednesday

- -

18
Thursday

- -

19
Friday

- -

20
Saturday

- -

Father's Day (US, UK)

21
Sunday

- -

Charming Windmills

This dynamic quilt from Pam and Nicky Lintott's *More Layer Cake, Jelly Roll & Charm Quilts* is made using two black print fabric charm packs and the authors' own choice of white tone-on-tone fabric. The Windmill block creates a sense of movement, and the positive/negative effect of the black and white fabric choice is very striking.

			JUNE			
M	T	W	T	F	S	S
1	2	3	4	5	6	7
8	9	10	11	12	13	14
15	16	17	18	19	20	21
22	23	24	25	26	27	28
29	30					

22
Monday

- -

23
Tuesday

- -

24
Wednesday

- -

25
Thursday

- -

26
Friday

- -

27
Saturday

- -

28
Sunday

- -

Mixed Fortunes

In *Quilt Colour Workshop*, the creative team behind the modern quilting e-zine, *Fat Quarterly*, unlock the secrets of colour theory and apply it to 12 modern quilt projects. This quilt, made by Brioni Greenberg, uses a wonderful collection of zingy yellows, green-yellows and orange-yellows. The dark background fabric adds the perfect contrast to this analogous colour scheme.

JUNE

M	T	W	T	F	S	S
1	2	3	4	5	6	7
8	9	10	11	12	13	14
15	16	17	18	19	20	21
22	23	24	25	26	27	28
29	30					

29
Monday

30
Tuesday

1
Wednesday

2
Thursday

Independence Day Observed (US)

3
Friday

Independence Day (US)

4
Saturday

5
Sunday

Beautiful Bow Ties

In *Antique to Heirloom Jelly Roll Quilts*, Pam and Nicky Lintott bring you 12 Jelly Roll™ quilt designs based on the best antique quilts in Pam's stunning collection of vintage quilts. This one is inspired by a gorgeous American quilt from the 1940s. Popular patterns used in quilts of this era include Delectable Mountains, Feathered Star and, of course, the beautiful Bow Tie.

JULY

M	T	W	T	F	S	S
		1	2	3	4	5
6	7	8	9	10	11	12
13	14	15	16	17	18	19
20	21	22	23	24	25	26
27	28	29	30	31		

6
Monday

7
Tuesday

8
Wednesday

9
Thursday

10
Friday

11
Saturday

12
Sunday

Marmalade Cake

All the designs in Pam and Nicky Lintott's *Dessert Roll Quilts*
can be made using just one Dessert Roll™, so you can be sure
that your fabrics will coordinate beautifully. As an extra treat
Pam and Nicky have included their family favourite dessert
recipes that inspired the quilt design themes. Their deliciously
moist marmalade cake makes the perfect teatime treat!

JULY

M	T	W	T	F	S	S
		1	2	3	4	5
6	7	8	9	10	11	12
13	14	15	16	17	18	19
20	21	22	23	24	25	26
27	28	29	30	31		

July

13
Monday

14
Tuesday

15
Wednesday

16
Thursday

17
Friday

18
Saturday

19
Sunday

Origami Runner

Quilt Colour Workshop provides many answers to the question:
What makes a great colour combination? The *Fat Quarterly* e-zine
team introduce you to the wonderful world of colour with 12
exciting quilt projects, including Brioni Greenberg's bright and
sophisticated runner which, with its analogous colour scheme,
uses blue and the two colours either side of it on the colour wheel.

			JULY			
M	T	W	T	F	S	S
			1	2	3	4	5
6	7	8	9	10	11	12
13	14	15	16	17	18	19
20	21	22	23	24	25	26
27	28	29	30	31		

July

20
Monday

21
Tuesday

22
Wednesday

23
Thursday

24
Friday

25
Saturday

26
Sunday

Cherry Ripe
This detail is taken from one of 12 designs featured in Lynne Edwards' book, *Blanket Stitch Quilts*. For the lovely cherry appliqués, several small-print red fabrics have been used. The cornerstone windmills on the sashing strips, made from the same fabric as the leaf appliqués, bring an energy to the finished quilt setting.

		JULY				
M	T	W	T	F	S	S
		1	2	3	4	5
6	7	8	9	10	11	12
13	14	15	16	17	18	19
20	21	22	23	24	25	26
27	28	29	30	31		

27
Monday

28
Tuesday

29
Wednesday

30
Thursday

31
Friday

1
Saturday

2
Sunday

Beach Huts and Gulls

Janet Clare, author of *Home Quilt Home*, has designed the perfect quilt to take to the beach on a summer's day. Simple and refreshingly coloured, it is big enough to lie on for a picnic and to wrap up in when the inevitable chill sets in, yet small enough to carry from the car. Best of all, it's quick to make and easily washed.

		AUGUST				
M	T	W	T	F	S	S
					1	2
3	4	5	6	7	8	9
10	11	12	13	14	15	16
17	18	19	20	21	22	23
24	25	26	27	28	29	30
31						

August

3
Monday

4
Tuesday

5
Wednesday

6
Thursday

7
Friday

8
Saturday

9
Sunday

Seaside Windmills

Lynne Edwards' book, *Cathedral Window Quilts*, provides a wealth of inspiration for exploring this classic folded technique, as well as variations on it. The Folded Windmill seen here is based on a Four-Patch block made from two layers of cut squares: the top layer of squares makes the windmill, the bottom layer the background.

AUGUST						
M	T	W	T	F	S	S
					1	2
3	4	5	6	7	8	9
10	11	12	13	14	15	16
17	18	19	20	21	22	23
24	25	26	27	28	29	30
31						

August

10
Monday

11
Tuesday

12
Wednesday

13
Thursday

14
Friday

15
Saturday

16
Sunday

Bajan Sunset

This beautiful quilt combines three different blocks, all containing flying geese units, half-square triangle units and squares, cut with the help of a Creative Grids Multi-Size Flying Geese Triangle ruler. It is one of 18 designs by Pam and Nicky Lintott in *Quick Quilts with Rulers* that explores quick and accurate cutting techniques for fast piecing.

AUGUST

M	T	W	T	F	S	S
					1	2
3	4	5	6	7	8	9
10	11	12	13	14	15	16
17	18	19	20	21	22	23
24	25	26	27	28	29	30
31						

August

17
Monday

18
Tuesday

19
Wednesday

20
Thursday

21
Friday

22
Saturday

23
Sunday

Feathers

Traditional designs like the chevron are easy to accomplish when worked the improv way as you don't have to worry about matching points! Lucie Summers, author of *Quilt Improv*, finds inspiration for her quilts everywhere, including on the Suffolk farm where she lives. This one was inspired by the distinctive markings of pheasant feathers and tractor tyre tracks.

AUGUST

M	T	W	T	F	S	S
					1	2
3	4	5	6	7	8	9
10	11	12	13	14	15	16
17	18	19	20	21	22	23
24	25	26	27	28	29	30
31						

24
Monday

25
Tuesday

26
Wednesday

27
Thursday

28
Friday

29
Saturday

30
Sunday

Scooter Strips

As the summer comes to an end, thoughts turn to the beginning of another college year. If you know someone who is looking to learn a new skill, there is no better place to start them off than with Elizabeth Betts' *Beginner's Guide to Quilting*. Full of easy and accessible projects, it updates even the most traditional of blocks – including Log Cabin – for a new generation of quilters.

		AUGUST				
M	T	W	T	F	S	S
					1	2
3	4	5	6	7	8	9
10	11	12	13	14	15	16
17	18	19	20	21	22	23
24	25	26	27	28	29	30
31						

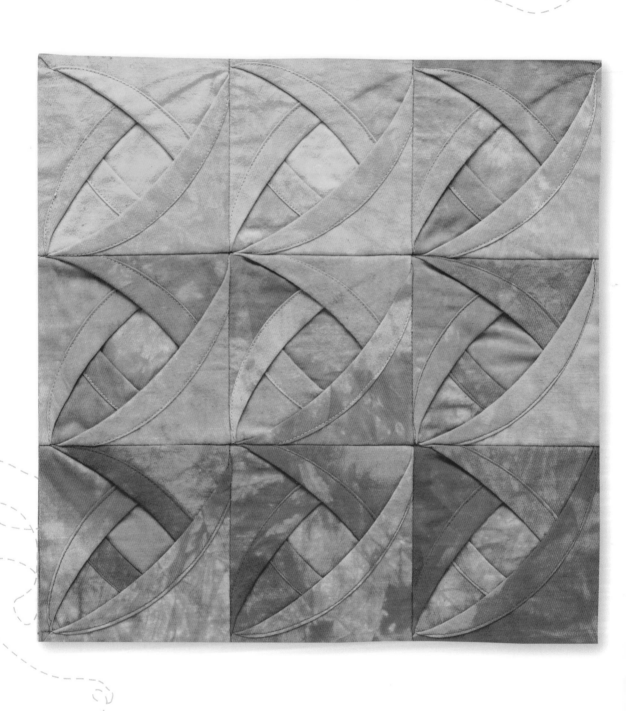

August/September

Summer Bank Holiday (UK)

31
Monday

1
Tuesday

2
Wednesday

3
Thursday

4
Friday

5
Saturday

Father's Day (Aus)

6
Sunday

Glowing Squares

Fabric folding techniques are greedy of fabric and can make for a very heavy quilt, so they are ideal for making little wall hangings like this one. A four-layer folded square is repeated in a nine-block design made in vivid colours, shaded in brightness from top left to bottom right. The aptly named Glowing Squares wall hanging can be found in Lynne Edwards' classic book, *Cathedral Window Quilts*.

SEPTEMBER

M	T	W	T	F	S	S
	1	2	3	4	5	6
7	8	9	10	11	12	13
14	15	16	17	18	19	20
21	22	23	24	25	26	27
28	29	30				

September

Labor Day (US)

7
Monday

8
Tuesday

9
Wednesday

10
Thursday

11
Friday

12
Saturday

13
Sunday

Railings

For this improv quilt, Lucie Summers wanted to create a sense
of looking through bars or railings, and in placing her fabrics
(an eclectic mix of fabric scraps, including tone-on-tones and
different scale prints) she hopes to give the impression of
glimpses of sky, trees and pavements. Lucie's book, *Quilt Improv*,
has a total of 12 stunning, contemporary quilts to explore.

SEPTEMBER

M	T	W	T	F	S	S
	1	2	3	4	5	6
7	8	9	10	11	12	13
14	15	16	17	18	19	20
21	22	23	24	25	26	27
28	29	30				

September

14
Monday

15
Tuesday

16
Wednesday

17
Thursday

18
Friday

19
Saturday

20
Sunday

Village Squares

Whether you are a city dweller or a country lover, you are sure to
find a quilt that will appeal to you in Janet Clare's, *Home Quilt Home*.
This single bed quilt was inspired by visits to friends who live deep
in the country, and the many country walks made through quiet
lanes, admiring the charming old cottages and imagining what life
would be like away from the hustle and bustle of the town.

SEPTEMBER						
M	T	W	T	F	S	S
	1	2	3	4	5	6
7	8	9	10	11	12	13
14	15	16	17	18	19	20
21	22	23	24	25	26	27
28	29	30				

September

21
Monday

22
Tuesday

23
Wednesday

24
Thursday

25
Friday

26
Saturday

27
Sunday

Cowslip Country

Quilt designer and workshop owner, Jo Colwill, firmly believes that recording your life in stitches is good for your soul. This cushion design from her book *Cushions & Quilts* depicts her love of horses, dogs, flowers, the countryside and quilts, and captures the beauty of the Cornish countryside where she works. The piecing and appliqué shapes can be easily adapted to suit your passions.

SEPTEMBER						
M	T	W	T	F	S	S
	1	2	3	4	5	6
7	8	9	10	11	12	13
14	15	16	17	18	19	20
21	22	23	24	25	26	27
28	29	30				

September/October

28
Monday

29
Tuesday

30
Wednesday

1
Thursday

2
Friday

3
Saturday

4
Sunday

OCTOBER						
M	T	W	T	F	S	S
			1	2	3	4
5	6	7	8	9	10	11
12	13	14	15	16	17	18
19	20	21	22	23	24	25
26	27	28	29	30	31	

Fracture

In *The Quilters' Guild Collection*, 12 award-winning quiltmakers were inspired by the traditional quilts at The Quilters' Guild Heritage Collection, to design their own contemporary pieces. Linda Kemshall's design turns the spotlight on crazy patchwork.

5
Monday

6
Tuesday

7
Wednesday

8
Thursday

9
Friday

10
Saturday

11
Sunday

OCTOBER						
M	T	W	T	F	S	S
			1	2	3	4
5	6	7	8	9	10	11
12	13	14	15	16	17	18
19	20	21	22	23	24	25
26	27	28	29	30	31	

Jubilee

The Double-Strip Kaleidoscope Ruler by Creative Grids is one of three rulers used by Pam and Nicky Lintott to create stunning quilt designs in *Quick Quilts with Rulers*. This quilt pattern, designed to celebrate Queen Elizabeth II's Diamond Jubilee, is a good one for using up assorted strips of fabric as the 'scrappy' effect works well.

October

Columbus Day (US)

12
Monday

13
Tuesday

14
Wednesday

15
Thursday

16
Friday

17
Saturday

18
Sunday

Autumnal Delights

There is a strong similarity between decorative floor tile layouts and traditional patchwork patterns, which Christine Porter explores in her book *Quilts Beneath Your Feet*. This design was inspired by a zigzag pattern seen in Bristol Cathedral, south west England, and it was made entirely with plaids, stripes and pieces of her husband's old shirt.

OCTOBER

M	T	W	T	F	S	S
			1	2	3	4
5	6	7	8	9	10	11
12	13	14	15	16	17	18
19	20	21	22	23	24	25
26	27	28	29	30	31	

19
Monday

20
Tuesday

21
Wednesday

22
Thursday

23
Friday

24
Saturday

25
Sunday

Calm Before the Storm

This quilt by Lynne Goldsworthy is a beautiful example of a red and white monotone quilt. Just two basic colours have been used to create the Mosaic blocks, but by utilizing so many scraps, this quilt really draws the eye. This is just one of 12 quilt designs exploring colour theory in *Quilt Colour Workshop*.

OCTOBER

M	T	W	T	F	S	S
			1	2	3	4
5	6	7	8	9	10	11
12	13	14	15	16	17	18
19	20	21	22	23	24	25
26	27	28	29	30	31	

October/November

26
Monday

27
Tuesday

28
Wednesday

29
Thursday

30
Friday

Halloween

31
Saturday

1
Sunday

Orange Squeeze

This quilt, made from just one Dessert Roll™, features
a simple Four-Patch block set on point with sashing and
sashing squares. Just add a few yards (metres) of background
fabric and you have a great bed-size quilt in no time at all.
Dessert Roll Quilts by Pam and Nicky Lintott has 12 designs,
with colour variations, for quick and easy quilting.

		NOVEMBER				
M	T	W	T	F	S	S
						1
2	3	4	5	6	7	8
9	10	11	12	13	14	15
16	17	18	19	20	21	22
23	24	25	26	27	28	29
30						

November

2
Monday

3
Tuesday

4
Wednesday

5
Thursday

6
Friday

7
Saturday

8
Sunday

Friday Night

This quilt was one of the first made by Pam and Nicky Lintott using the Double-Strip Kaleidoscope Ruler by Creative Grids, and it was love at first cut! So much so that they followed it up with a larger variation made one Saturday morning, which you can find in their book, *Quick Quilts with Rulers*.

NOVEMBER						
M	T	W	T	F	S	S
						1
2	3	4	5	6	7	8
9	10	11	12	13	14	15
16	17	18	19	20	21	22
23	24	25	26	27	28	29
30						

November

9
Monday

10
Tuesday

Veterans Day (US)

11
Wednesday

12
Thursday

13
Friday

14
Saturday

15
Sunday

Masu Stacking Boxes

The simplicity of a square in a square is used in this lovely quilt, echoing the pattern formed by *masu*, which were stacking boxes once used to measure rice in Japan. All the quilts featured in Susan Briscoe's *Japanese Quilt Inspirations* are based on traditional motifs to allow you to present your Japanese fabrics in an authentic style.

			NOVEMBER			
M	T	W	T	F	S	S
						1
2	3	4	5	6	7	8
9	10	11	12	13	14	15
16	17	18	19	20	21	22
23	24	25	26	27	28	29
30						

November

16
Monday

17
Tuesday

18
Wednesday

19
Thursday

20
Friday

21
Saturday

22
Sunday

Dancing Stars

More Layer Cake, Jelly Roll & Charm Quilts by Pam and Nicky Lintott is a book that is dedicated to providing ingenious ideas for using pre-cut fabric collections with little or no waste. The dancing stars that give this quilt its name are formed from flip-over corners made from different sized squares, which almost makes them look as if they are twinkling!

		NOVEMBER				
M	T	W	T	F	S	S
						1
2	3	4	5	6	7	8
9	10	11	12	13	14	15
16	17	18	19	20	21	22
23	24	25	26	27	28	29
30						

November

23
Monday

24
Tuesday

25
Wednesday

Thanksgiving (US)

26
Thursday

27
Friday

28
Saturday

29
Sunday

Pinwheel Paradise

Quilt pattern designer Laura Coons was delighted when Pam and Nicky Lintott chose not one, but two of her quilt designs to be included in their book *Jelly Roll Dreams*, a collection of the 12 winning quilts from the Jelly Roll™ Dream Challenge. She was inspired to make Pinwheel Paradise when she fell in love with some candy batiks, and the linking effect she has created for the square frames is very clever.

NOVEMBER

M	T	W	T	F	S	S
						1
2	3	4	5	6	7	8
9	10	11	12	13	14	15
16	17	18	19	20	21	22
23	24	25	26	27	28	29
30						

30
Monday

1
Tuesday

2
Wednesday

3
Thursday

4
Friday

5
Saturday

6
Sunday

Advent Calendar

Christmas is coming, so get in the mood with this lovely advent calendar quilt. It has 24 houses each with a special little charm hanging behind the three-dimensional door. As you count down the days to Christmas, the charms can be removed and hung on the appliqué tree. A free quilt pattern sheet for the advent calendar is included in Jo Colwill's book, *Cushions & Quilts*.

DECEMBER

M	T	W	T	F	S	S
	1	2	3	4	5	6
7	8	9	10	11	12	13
14	15	16	17	18	19	20
21	22	23	24	25	26	27
28	29	30	31			

December

7
Monday

8
Tuesday

9
Wednesday

10
Thursday

11
Friday

12
Saturday

13
Sunday

Bricks and Fences

Lucie Summers, author of *Quilt Improv*, was inspired to make this quilt by the most everyday of objects — some holes in a fence in her garden and brick pathways in a public garden. The resulting design combines two dynamic shapes, portholes and half-square triangles, to great effect.

DECEMBER

M	T	W	T	F	S	S
	1	2	3	4	5	6
7	8	9	10	11	12	13
14	15	16	17	18	19	20
21	22	23	24	25	26	27
28	29	30	31			

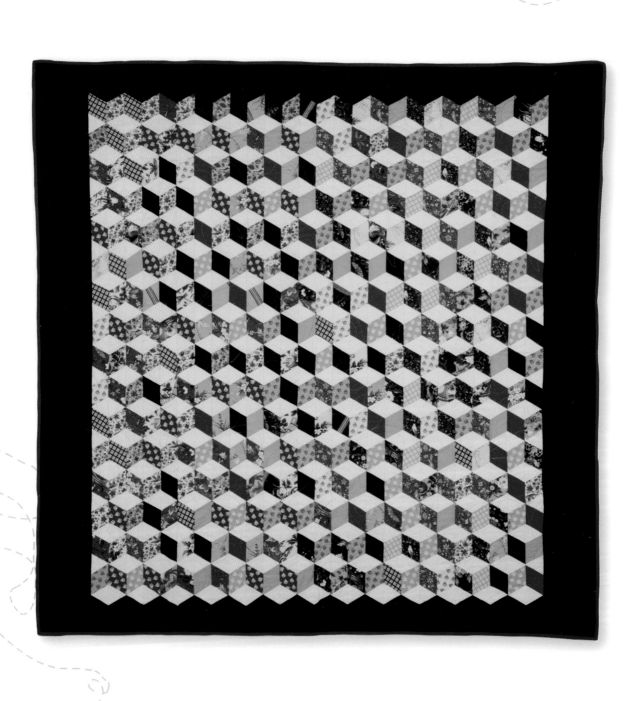

December

14
Monday

15
Tuesday

16
Wednesday

17
Thursday

18
Friday

19
Saturday

20
Sunday

Tumbling Blocks

The three-dimensional effect of Tumbling Blocks is made by selecting the correct mix of dark, medium and light fabrics. Inspired by a vintage quilt made by three generations of one family, this is just one of 12 new Jelly Roll™ designs to appear in Pam and Nicky Lintott's *Antique to Heirloom Jelly Roll Quilts*, featuring patterns based on their incredible collection of vintage quilts.

			DECEMBER			
M	T	W	T	F	S	S
	1	2	3	4	5	6
7	8	9	10	11	12	13
14	15	16	17	18	19	20
21	22	23	24	25	26	27
28	29	30	31			

December

21
Monday

22
Tuesday

23
Wednesday

24
Thursday

Christmas Day

25
Friday

Boxing Day (UK, Aus)

26
Saturday

27
Sunday

Little Deer Duo

Desperate to brighten up your home before family and friends descend on you for Christmas? Why not make a simple patchwork cushion for the guest bedroom or a hanging decoration for the tree, both decorated with a sweet little deer appliqué? Helen Philipps' *Pretty Patchwork Gifts* features over 25 easy-stitch patchwork projects that are perfect for giving, whatever the occasion.

DECEMBER

M	T	W	T	F	S	S
	1	2	3	4	5	6
7	8	9	10	11	12	13
14	15	16	17	18	19	20
21	22	23	24	25	26	27
28	29	30	31			

December /January

Bank Holiday (UK, Aus)

28
Monday

29
Tuesday

30
Wednesday

31
Thursday

New Year's Day

1
Friday

2
Saturday

3
Sunday

Trade Winds

What a fantastic setting for this stunning quilt. The colours may be
seasonal red and green, but the setting is decidedly tropical. The
Trade Winds quilt, which can be found in Pam and Nicky Lintott's
book *Quick Quilts with Rulers*, will help you to perfect your Flying
Geese units, made large for the blocks and small for the border.

JANUARY 2016						
M	T	W	T	F	S	S
				1	2	3
4	5	6	7	8	9	10
11	12	13	14	15	16	17
18	19	20	21	22	23	24
25	26	27	28	29	30	31

Useful Information

It is hoped that the quilt photographs featured in this diary have inspired you to take your own quilt skills further. Wherever you are located, there are bound to be opportunities for you to see other quilters' work and to share your love of this amazing textile art. Use the following information to help you find out what is going on near you.

UK
Organizations

The Quilters' Guild of the British Isles is an independent registered educational charity with over 7,000 members. www.quiltersguild.org.uk

Exhibitions

The Festival of Quilts
Billed as the ultimate patchwork and quilting experience, this event, run collaboratively between Twisted Thread and the Quilters Guild of the British Isles, is the largest quilt show in Europe with over 30,000 visitors each year. A four-day show held in August at the National Exhibition Centre, Birmingham, it has over 1,000 competition quilts on display, as well as galleries from leading international quilt artists and groups. There are over 300 exhibitors selling specialist patchwork and quilting supplies, plus hundreds of masterclasses, workshops and lectures.
www.thefestivalofquilts.co.uk

Quilts UK
The organizers of this exhibition, Grosvenor Shows Ltd, hold several patchwork and quilting exhibitions nationally each year. The largest of these is Quilts UK held in May at the Three Counties Showground in the beautiful Malvern Hills in Worcestershire. The longest established show in the UK, it attracts over 9,000 visitors annually. It is an open competitive show with over 400 quilts on display and 150 trade stands.
www.grosvenorshows.co.uk

The National Quilt Championships
An open competitive quilt show held at Sandown Park in June attracting over 5,000 visitors. Over 400 quilts are on display, including features from well-known artists from the UK and overseas, incorporating a mix of traditional and contemporary quilts.
www.grosvenorshows.co.uk

Spring and Autumn Quilt Festivals
A number of smaller, local quilt shows are also organized by Grosvenor Shows Ltd. Locations include: Ardingly, Duxford, Edinburgh, Exeter, Maidstone and Malvern.
www.grosvenorshows.co.uk

Quiltfest
Quiltfest's aim is to showcase the cutting edge of textile design and making, and to enable quiltmakers in Wales and the Northwest of England to see work that may not normally be exhibited in the region. It is an annual show held in February at the Royal International Pavilion in North Wales. www.quiltfest.org.uk

USA
Organizations

American Quilter's Society (AQS)
The aim of the AQS is to provide a forum for quilters of all skill levels to expand their horizons in quiltmaking, design, self-expression and quilt collecting. It publishes books and magazines, has product offers, and runs quilt shows and contests, workshops and other activities.
www.americanquilter.com

The International Quilting Association (IQA)
The IQA is a non-profit organization dedicated to the preservation of the art of quilting, the attainment of public recognition for quilting as an art form, and the advancement of the state of the art throughout the world. Founded in 1979, it supports many quilting projects and activities, and organizes three consumer shows and two trade shows each year at various major city venues in the USA.
www.quilts.com

Exhibitions

American Quilter's Society Quilt Shows
The AQS organizes a number of quilt shows annually throughout the USA. For more details visit their website.
www.americanquilter.com

The International Quilting Association Quilt Shows
Quilts, Inc., the IQA's exhibiton arm, holds three consumer shows (International Quilt Festival and Quilt! Knit! Stitch!) and two trade shows (International Quilt Market) annually.
www.quilts.com

Sisters Outdoor Quilt Show
This is the largest outdoor quilt show in the world with over 12,500 attendees and is held on the second Saturday of July in Sisters, Oregon.
www.sistersoutdoorquiltshow.org

The Mancuso Quilt Shows
Mancuso Show Management, run by brothers David and Peter Mancuso, promotes seven major national and international quilting and textile arts festivals held across the USA.
www.quiltfest.com

CANADA
Organizations

Canadian Quilters' Association
Formed in 1981, the aims and objectives of the Canadian Quilters' Association are: to promote a greater understanding, appreciation, and knowledge of the art, techniques, and heritage of patchwork, appliqué, and quilting; to promote the highest standards of workmanship and design in both traditional and innovative work; and to foster cooperation and sharing among quiltmakers. There are a number of Canadian Quilters' Association sponsored events including the National Juried Show (NJS), Canada's most prestigious quilt show.
www.canadianquilter.com

AUSTRALIA
Organizations

The Quilters' Guild of NSW
A Sydney-based organization which aims to promote the art and craft of patchwork and quilting. Membership is open to anyone with an interest in the craft, from the beginner to the professional, and it has over 1,000 members.
www.quiltersguildnsw.com

Quilters' Guild of South Australia
This organization has over 500 individual guild members with over 100 city and country groups now affiliated with the guild.
www.saquilters.org.au

Exhibitions

Australia's No.1 Craft and Quilt Fairs
Expertise Events run several craft and quilting fairs in Australia (Perth, Sydney, Launceston – Tasmania, Melbourne, Canberra, Brisbane, Adelaide) and New Zealand (Christchurch, Hamilton and Palmerston North).
www.craftfair.com.au

The Australasian Quilt Convention (AQC)
Held in Melbourne, this is Australia's largest annual quilt-dedicated event, incorporating classes and lectures with highly skilled tutors, much-anticipated social events, a shopping market plus exhibitor workshops and exclusive quilt displays. It brings together thousands of quilters from all over Australia and around the world.
www.aqc.com.au

NEW ZEALAND
Organizations

Aotearoa National Association of New Zealand Quilters
Formed in 1994 as the National Association of New Zealand Quilters (NANZQ) the principle objective is to promote and lead the development of patchwork, quilting and textile artists within New Zealand.
www.aotearoaquilters.co.nz

More About the Quilts

The quilts included in the *Quilter's Desk Diary 2015* have all been selected from the great range of patchwork and quilting books published by David & Charles. If you would like to find out more about any of the quilt designs featured, why not treat yourself to a few of these great books. For more information about these and other high-quality craft books visit: **www.stitchcraftcreate.co.uk**

Antique to Heirloom Jelly Roll Quilts
Pam & Nicky Lintott

ISBN-13: 978-1-4463-0182-1

Twelve new Jelly Roll™ quilt designs based on the best antique quilts from Pam Lintott's stunning vintage collection. Each clever quilt pattern uses just one Jelly Roll™.

Beginner's Guide to Quilting
Elizabeth Betts

ISBN-13: 978-1-4463-0254-5

Learn all the quilting basics, from paper piecing to appliqué to hand and machine quilting. Features 16 simple projects, from bags and cushions to wall hangings and quilts.

Blanket Stitch Quilts
Lynne Edwards

ISBN-13: 978-1-4463-0136-4

Learn to sew beautiful handmade quilts with simple blanket stitch appliqué technique. Choose from 12 inspiring projects.

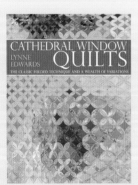

Cathedral Window Quilts
Lynne Edwards

ISBN-13: 978-0-7153-2713-5

Explore classic techniques using fabulous fabrics to create over 25 flamboyantly folded projects, ranging from heirloom quilts and striking wall hangings to colourful, quick-to-make cushions, bags and pincushions.

Cushions & Quilts
Jo Colwill

ISBN-13: 978-1-4463-0256-9

A collection of 20 projects for a range of cushions and quilts, all inspired by Jo Colwill's life on her Cornish farm. Includes Jo's trademark cushion styles and features all her quilting and sewing tips and advice.

Features a full sized pattern for the Advent Calender Quilt.

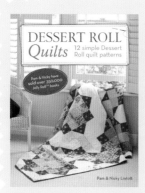

Dessert Roll Quilts
Pam & Nicky Lintott

ISBN-13: 978-1-4463-0354-2

Twelve quilt patterns provide inspiration for beginners and experienced quilters, using the latest Dessert Roll™ pre-cut fabrics from Moda.

Easy Japanese Quilt Style
Julia Davis & Anne Muxworthy

ISBN-13: 978-0-7153-2862-0

The perfect book for quilters of all abilities who want to introduce Japanese style into their homes with ingenious quick-to-stitch projects, ranging from bags to wall hangings.

The Essential Sampler Quilt Book
Lynne Edwards

ISBN-13: 978-0-7153-3613-7

Masterclass instruction from the sampler quilt expert for making 40 pieced blocks using both hand and machine techniques, with a wealth of quilt photographs to inspire colour and fabric choices.

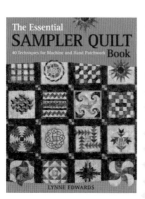

Floral Dimensions
Pauline Ineson

ISBN-13: 978-1-4463-0181-4

Features 20 gorgeous dimensional flowers cleverly manipulated in fabric, including the daffodil, marigold, rose and tulip, and derived from the author's incredible multi-award winning quilt.

Home Quilt Home
Janet Clare

ISBN-13: 978-0-4463-0377-1

An inspiring collection of designs for quilts, wall hangings and cushions, all based around the idea of 'the home'. Designs to choose from include townhouses, quaint cottages and seaside beach huts.

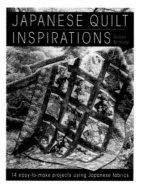

Japanese Quilt Inspirations
Susan Briscoe

ISBN-13: 978-0-7153-3827-8

Ten stunning quilt designs that make clever use of fabric favourites such as fat quarters, strip rolls and feature panels, as well as kimono widths and furoshiki (wrapping cloths).

Japanese Sashiko Inspirations
Susan Briscoe

ISBN-13: 978-0-7153-2641-4

Discover sashiko, the Japanese method of decorative stitching to create striking patterns on fabric with lines of simple running stitch. Bring a touch of the Orient to your home with over 25 projects to choose from.

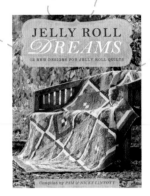

Jelly Roll Dreams
Pam & Nicky Lintott

ISBN-13: 978-1-4463-0040-4

A stunning showcase for the 12 winning quilts from the 2011 Jelly Roll Dream Challenge, each made from just one Jelly Roll™, with variations provided by Pam & Nicky Lintott.

Making Welsh Quilts
Mary Jenkins & Clare Claridge

ISBN-13: 978-0-7153-2996-2

This book explores the fascinating history of Welsh quilting and features 10 sumptuous projects for you to make in the traditional style, using strikingly simple patchwork designs and decorative quilting patterns.

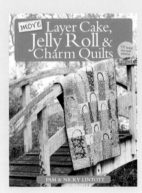

More Layer Cake, Jelly Roll & Charm Quilts
Pam & Nicky Lintott

ISBN-13: 978-0-7153-3898-8

A second helping of 14 brand new quilt designs to help quilters get the most from favourite pre-cut fabric bundles, for quilts that are quick to piece and a joy to make.

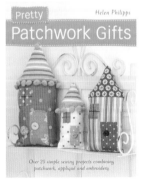

Pretty Patchwork Gifts
Helen Philipps

ISBN-13: 978-1-4463-0213-2

Over 25 simple sewing projects that combine patchwork, appliqué and embroidery, from corsages and purses to bags and cushions.

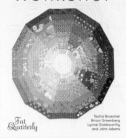

Quilt Colour Workshop
Fat Quarterly: Tacha Bruecher, Brioni Greenberg, Lynne Goldsworthy and John Adams

ISBN-13: 978-1-4463-0375-7

A practical guide to using colour in your quilting projects from the members of Fat Quarterly, the popular e-zine on modern quilting.

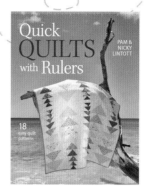

Quick Quilt with Rulers
Pam & Nicky Lintott

ISBN-13: 978-1-4463-0469-3

A collection of 18 stunning quilt designs made using one of three rulers for quick and easy patchwork.

Quilts Beneath Your Feet
Christine Porter

ISBN-13: 978-0-7153-3293-1

An exciting collection of 10 original pieced patchwork quilt designs together with variation ideas, all inspired by traditional floor tiles from churches, cathedrals and historic buildings around the world.

The Quilters' Guild Collection
Editor: Bridget Long

ISBN-13: 978-0-7153-2668-8

The Quilters' Guild Heritage Collection is the largest collection of patchwork and quilting in the UK, dating back as far as the 18th century. Twelve contemporary quiltmakers each take inspiration from heritage pieces to make a project for today.

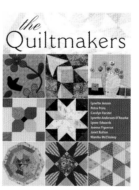

The Quiltmakers
Consultant Editor: Pam Lintott

ISBN-13: 978-0-7153-3173-6

A unique opportunity to take eight masterclasses from some of the very best quilters in the world, without ever leaving home. Topics include creating perspective, perfect piecing, and inspired fabric collage.

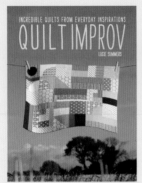

Quilt Improv
Lucie Summers

ISBN-13: 978-1-4463-0294-1

Discover how to use
improvisational methods
to create 12 stunning
contemporary quilts and
develop your own designs.

Tessellation Quilts
Christine Porter

ISBN-13: 978-0-7153-1941-3

Discover how you can
translate simple interlocking
patterns into stunning pieced
patchwork designs. Nine
tessellating block designs
are explored in detail, with
over 45 quilts illustrating
how the blocks can be used
in very different ways.

Two from One Jelly
Roll Quilts
Pam & Nicky Lintott

ISBN-13: 978-0-7153-3756-1

Learn how to make two
different quilts using just
one Jelly Roll™ – half the
fabric, twice the inspiration.
It features 18 patterns to
help you make your fabric
go further.

More About the Quiltmakers

The quilt designs featured in *The Quilter's Desk Diary 2015* showcase the talents of some of the world's most respected and creative quiltmakers. The names of those whose work is included are listed below.

Elizabeth Betts runs her Brighton-based quilting shop, Quilty Pleasures, with her mother, Susan. *Beginner's Guide to Quilting* is her first book.
www.quilty-pleasures.co.uk

Janet Bolton has written two books for children as well as several books on her appliqué and quilting techniques. Her work is represented in the collections of the Crafts Council, British Council and the Embroiderer's Guild.
www.janetbolton.com

Susan Briscoe was introduced to sashiko while teaching English in Japan. Susan's sashiko designs have been published in *Popular Patchwork, British Patchwork & Quilting* and *Fabrications*, and she has written over ten books on quilting.
www.susanbriscoe.co.uk

Janet Clare is an established quilting and sewing tutor and author. She is a fabric designer for Moda, a regular attendee of Festival of Quilts and teaches workshops for quilt groups throughout the UK.
www.janetclare.co.uk

Clare Claridge is a world expert on Welsh quilting patterns, and she is the co-author of *Making Welsh Quilts* along with **Mary Jenkins**, a collector of Welsh quilts and samplers.

Jo Colwill runs her shop and workshop space, Cowslip Workshops, from her organic farm in Launceston, Cornwall. She has been quilting and teaching for over 20 years and is highly respected in the quilting community.
www.cowslipworkshops.co.uk

Laura Coons, Jennifer Goldstein, and **Joanna Wilczynska** were all finalists in the 2011 Jelly Roll™

Dream Challenge.

Julia Davis and **Anne Muxworthy** run the Step By Step Patchwork Centre in South Molton, Devon. They specialize in Japanese fabrics, and offer several kits that make great use of them.
www.stepbystep-quilts.co.uk

Lynne Edwards specializes in sampler quilts and the cathedral window technique. She has been the recipient of many prestigious awards including the Jewel Pearce Patterson Scholarship for International Quilt Teachers and the Amy Emms Memorial Trophy. In 2008 she was awarded an MBE for services to Arts and Crafts.

Joanna Figueroa is a talented designer and quiltmaker and founder of Fig Tree & Co. Joanna designs the gorgeous Fig Tree fabrics for Moda fabrics. She has published over 100 quilting, sewing and children's patterns and design booklets.
www.figtreeandco.com

Lynne Goldsworthy is one of four founding members of Fat Quarterly, an online modern quilting and sewing magazine run by a group of modern quilters.
www.fatquarterly.com

Brioni Greenberg is one of the Fat Quarterly team. Brioni met her fellow team members – **Tacha Bruecher, Lynne Goldsworthy** and **John Adams** – via various online quilting bees and swaps. Through Fat Quarterly they hope to make the world one huge quilting bee.
www.fatquarterly.com

Pauline Ineson is an award-winning quilter who specializes in machine sewing and appliqué techniques. She has taught machine sewing courses for over 10 years, and these include

the Heirloom Quilt and Appliqué Quilt courses.
www.paulineineson.co.uk

Linda Kemshall works together with her daughter Laura Kemshall as DesignMatters, an online teaching resource for their innovative approach to textiles. They also run DesignMatters TV, a web-based subscription TV service covering all the creative techniques used in their artwork.
www.lindakemshall.com

Pam Lintott and **Nicky Lintott** run The Quilt Room in Dorking, Surrey. Pam's first book, *The Quilt Room*, was a compilation of work from the very best patchworkers. Pam has also written several books with daughter Nicky, whose main focus is on developing their longarm quilting business.
www.quiltroom.co.uk

Helen Philipps studied printed textiles and embroidery at Manchester Metropolitan University before becoming a freelance designer. Her work regularly features in popular craft magazines.
www.helenphilipps.blogspot.co.uk

Christine Porter teaches, lectures and judges in the US, Canada, Europe and the Middle East. She is also the British coordinator for the World Quilt and Textile competition. **www.christineporterquilts.com**

Lucie Summers, a graduate from the Norwich School of Art & Design, sells her distinctive hand-printed fabrics under the label Summersville. She also designs for Moda Fabrics and has written many magazine articles about her work.
www.blu-shed.blogspot.com

Creative Quilting

For Patchwork and
Quilting supplies
Workshops and Classes to suit all
levels Open 7 days a week Secure
Online Ordering

www.creativequilting.co.uk
Facebook Page: Creative Quilting

Pinterest: Creative Quilting

cosy café
fantastic fabric shop
exclusive nicholas mosse pottery
classes & workshops
plenty of inspiration
we look forward to
welcoming you soon.........

Shop open
Mon - Sat 9.00am - 5.00pm
(Sun 10.00am - 4.00pm)

food@cowslip open everyday
10.00am - 4.30pm
(closed Christmas/New Year)

COWSLIP WORKSHOPS

Newhouse Farm, St. Stephens,
Launceston PL15 8JX
01566 772 654
info@cowslipworkshops.co.uk
www.cowslipworkshops.com

A DAVID & CHARLES BOOK
© F&W Media International, Ltd 2014

David & Charles is an imprint of F&W Media International, Ltd
Brunel House, Forde Close, Newton Abbot, TQ12 4PU, UK

F&W Media International, Ltd is a subsidiary of F+W Media, Inc
10151 Carver Road, Suite #200 Blue Ash, OH 45242, USA

Text and layout © F&W Media International, Ltd 2014

Photography © F&W Media International, Ltd 2014
(except 16, 66, 82, 90 and 106 © Pam & Nicky Lintott 2014)

First published in the UK and USA in 2014

A catalogue record for this book is available from the British Library.

ISBN-13: 978-1-4463-0490-7 hardback
ISBN-10: 1-4463-0490-6 hardback

Printed in China by Toppan Leefung Printing Limited for:
F&W Media International, Ltd
Brunel House, Forde Close, Newton Abbot, TQ12 4PU, UK

Front cover quilt designed by Lynne Goldsworthy, photographed by Jack Gorman and Jack Kirby from BangWallop for *Quilt Colour Workshop* (Tacha Bruecher, Brioni Greenberg, Lynne Goldsworthy and John Adams, 2014).

Back cover quilt designed by Lucie Summers, photographed by Mark Scott for *Quilt Improv* (Lucie Summers, 2014).

F+W Media publishes high quality books on a wide range of subjects.
For more great book ideas visit: **www.stitchcraftcreate.co.uk**